Ian Ritchie   LIFE

UNICORN

Ian Ritchie leads ritchie*studio, one of the world's most innovative and influential contemporary architectural practices, based in London.

He also co-founded the design engineering practice Rice Francis Ritchie (aka RFR) in Paris which contributed to several of President Mitterrand's 'Grands Projets' including the Louvre Pyramids and Sculpture Courts, and La Villette Cité des Sciences.

Ian is a Royal Academician and a member of the Akademie der Künste in Berlin. He is an Honorary Fellow of the Royal Academy of Music and Royal Academy of Engineering, and Fellow of the Royal Society of Arts and Society of Façade Engineering.

He is advisor to the Backstage Trust, member of Milan Polytechnic's Urbanism, Architecture and Construction Academic Board, and has been adviser to the British Museum, Natural History Museum, The Ove Arup Foundation, President of Columbia University, and the Centre for Urban Science and Progress NYU.

He has chaired international juries including RIBA Stirling Prize, French Govt. Jeunes Albums, Czech Architecture Grand Prix and the Berlin Art Prize.

His art is held in several international galleries, museums and private collections.

Introduction	4
Youth	6
Love	12
Art	18
Architecture	24
Our Planet	32
Covid	44
War & Peace	50
Lost Friends	56

Introduction

The only life we know is the one that exists within the biosphere of our planet.

And as many of us have known since the 1970s, in the complex interplay between humanity and our planet, a delicate equilibrium hangs in the balance. Our biosphere is in distress because Earth's overall albedo – measured by the amount of solar energy absorbed and emitted from Earth's surface – is being subtly modulated by the composition of the atmosphere that surrounds the planet. As carbon dioxide levels increase, absorbing and re-emitting more of the sun's energy in the form of infra-red radiation, the planet's surface temperature is increasing over the long term.

In the second chapter, 'Architecture, Ecology and Global Economics', of my first book, *(well) Connected Architecture*, I speculated on the implications of our interdependence.

A new wider and more appreciative Europe is, hopefully, not simply the creation in the coming years of the largest, most powerful single economic market that the world has ever seen, but a staging post, symbolic of a desire to achieve a more integrated whole world . . . The Earth owes man nothing.

This collection *is* more than a personal journey. It is also a plea to transcend conventional thinking and embrace the interconnectedness of all things. During the past fifty years, our shortsightedness has undermined the potential for a global appreciation of the climate threat and blinded us to the fact that we all share the same air and water. As human civilisation faces an existential environmental crisis, exacerbated by political short-termism and wilful ignorance, we seem to be moving politically further away than ever from a global consensus on climate.

Yet I remain optimistic. Just as throughout my life I have always sought to express our relationship with the natural world through the transformative power of architecture and art, I am convinced that we will come to understand the transformative potential within our grasp, developing ways to allow human life to be in harmony within the biosphere and in the process redefining the way humankind views its place on the Earth – an Earth that will be quite different from the one my generation has known.

IAN RITCHIE, LONDON, FEBRUARY 2024

This is the final book of the trilogy, *Li*nes, *Li*ght and *Li*fe, and includes poems from 1965-2024

Li – 理 is a concept found in neo-Confucian Chinese philosophy underlying reason and order of nature

YOUTH

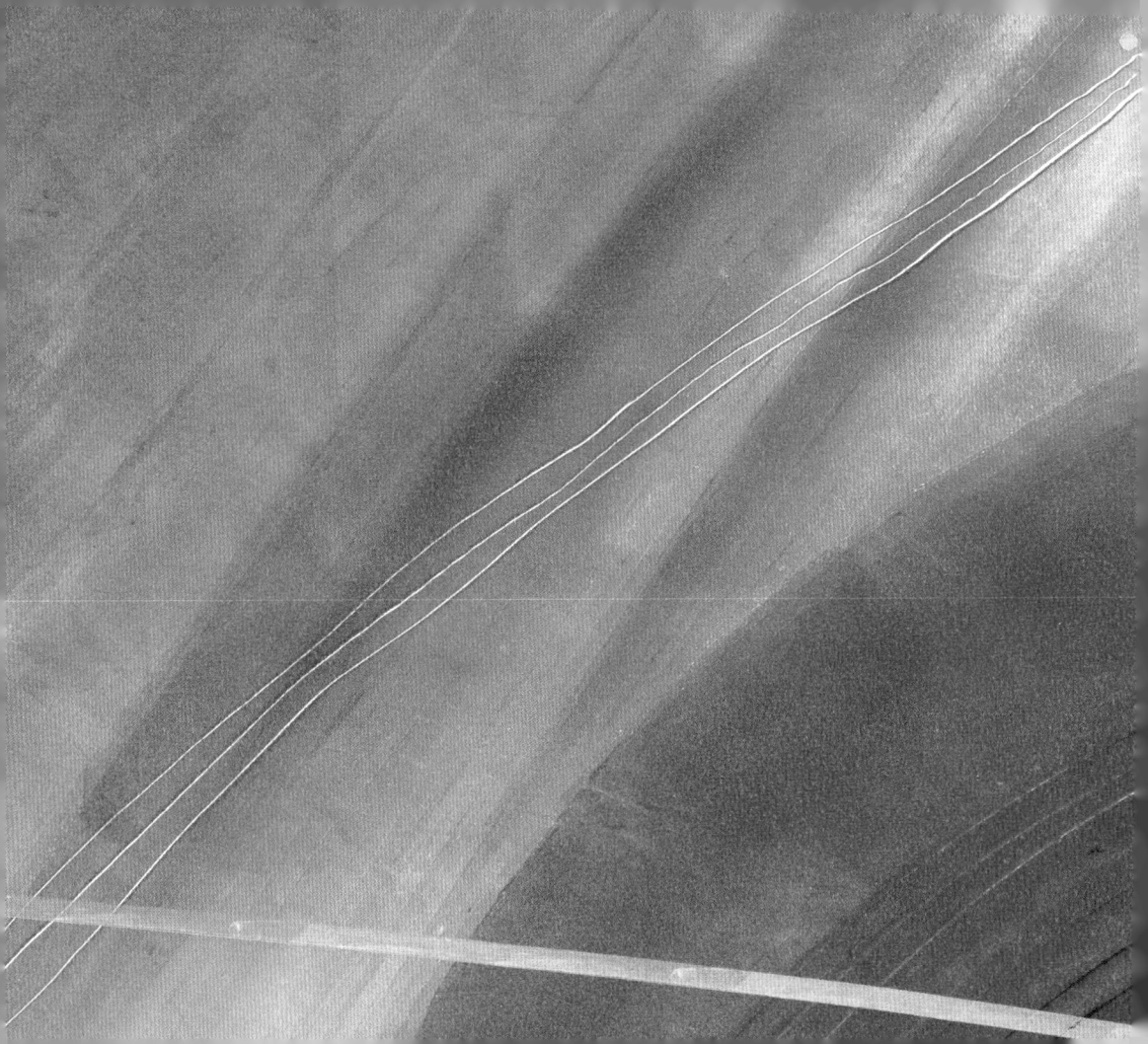

Life

Life feels like emptying the sea
    from the seashore
    with a seashell.
While you are on the seashore
    with me I am happy
      playing with the sand
      instead of the sea.

The unselfish home

This is where our hearts live.
    Indivisible from the footsteps of home,
    rhythmic beat of life,
    habits filling spaces.
We share, copy, adopt,
    adapt, accumulate and make things, events,
    until that time when richness is the family,
    the one composed of us.
We line our walls with art,
    our shelves with books and glass desks
    with photos,
    now in the digital age
    DVDs and downloads.
So very intimate,
    a protected world of smells and special
    words,
    familiar sounds of rain
    and patterns of sunlight.

We know which way is south,
    the direction of the wind along our street,
    where the blackbird is
    when singing at twilight.
Thinking of doors to rooms
    as if they were lips that could tell stories
    of life behind them,
    of murmured memories.
Home, as love nurtures life,
    and where laughing, tasting, touching
    and seeing
    bring self-awareness
    and shape our being.

Quark!

Following the five-letter word game
    my world will never be the same.
    Flying across brown Siberia
    towards Japan and Oita.
Unlearn the holy trinity
    of old bonded connectivity,
    of Neutron, Proton and Electron
    another strange phenomenon.
I must talk to my molecules
    in order to work out these new rules
    "Are you just the same, my dear Neutron?"
    "Apparently not, my dear Proton"
"Now we've got three brand-new babies
    inside our sub-atomic arteries"
    "Hello one Up, one Down, and one
    Strange Quark"
    Joyce's Three Quarks for Master Mark?!
Now, back in equilibrium
    Despite yesterday's delirium.
    "Can't see any electrons today,
    Have the Quarks pushed'em all away?"

One more time

One more time
    may I hold your hand
    just one more time?
Will our cheeks touch
    just one more time?
and that soft embrace
    maybe one more time?
My hand on your thigh
    accidentally again?
That rushed goodnight kiss
    is it still possible?

LOVE

Can I write of Love

As the pen is the tongue of the mind,
   so a kiss is the song of the heart.

A Word About Love

More words have been written
   about love than any other subject.
   And every man and woman smitten
   remains suspect, even circumspect,
   except those, like us, who understand,
   and feel without question, love expand.

Harbour 2

Where is my harbour
    and my boat safe –
    held from anxious cries of
    life's weather?
There, resting, safely
    wrapped by lines of rope
    held, as if dancing
    to the wave-lengths.
In this mon amour
    my heart is your world
    held, yet floating free,
    on waves that fold
In a temporal warp that
    we know separates
    the very togetherness
    that the sunshine joins.

In Black Ink

That in black ink
    my love may still shine bright.
Although ephemeral,
    fugitive in this ethereal form
    of electrons on the screen,
    the spirit of black resides
    in the words that mean so much.
One day soon, in black ink,
    my love will be
    permanently inscribed.

Nothing and Everything

There are only a few people
    you meet in life, who,
    even when they say nothing,
    say everything.

Dancing Now

I walked along the edge of the river,
    my breath white against the reddening sky.
    And as the gulls followed the boat
    your silhouette, your smile, caught my eye.
I stopped, transfixed, the moon so full,
    so round,
    my heart warmed, leapt and defrosting
    the air
    close to my body, conjured more images.
I was dancing now, you with me, I swear.

Alchemist

I felt closer to you than ever before.
    Neither the Alchemist on his white steed
    nor the desert men in black,
    could stretch their necks to where
    my imagined hand rested on your heart,
    or when my cheek lay on your bosom.
The ethereal azzurra blue today
    lies above me, with you
    now a distant blanket on the sand.

Yes, and Yes Again

The words are my colours,
    poems my paintings.
Our letters are our passion,
    our world's full of rainbows.

ART

Twilight

[to Richard England 2014]

You touched my soul!
I am not sure, ever,
    if life sustains the soul
    or,
    the soul sustains life,
    but moments with you
    my dear friend,
    dance between the two.
We are in the twilight.
    Does light sustain life
    or,
    life reveal light?
    For the poem, thank you
    for the gift
    of time and thoughts too.

All Art Has Structure …

Painting, poetry
    sculpture, architecture
    literature, theatre and music.
Oh! How beautiful life is.
Yet, thinking of those who will be
    hungry and cold in winter.
        One kind word will warm three winter months.
Say it to those you love.

Time to Write

Time to write a poem
    and to feed the snowmen
    their carrot noses
    and their prune eyes.
It is summer but winter
    thoughts are still allowed.

Until

I prefer to slip into my mind
    to see lakes lying like deflated clouds,
    and reflecting until my ideas
    can be set free to float
    upon the winds of the world
    and to be shared.

Poems

Where do poems come from?
    They come from silence, from the air,
    from nowhere and everywhere.
    They arrive, just as colours find the artist.
Blank canvas in your mind,
    paper on a table indoors,
    or held carefully outdoors.
    The setting framed, empty except the noises.
In the mental silence
    the poem erases on that page,
    words, too many words to gauge
    preventing much better ones arriving.
Mind of infinity,
    the clouds and sounds and memories
    pass in the silence and emptiness
    while coaxing words to settle as a poem.

Reflection on Art Poem 1 (Extract)

I cherish liberty if it means
    that we are honest and open.
If transparency is like the sun's rays
    and information real,
    and we all share it equally
    then liberty is possible.
If we distort either or both,
    liberty is dead and
    a world of wolves howling
    will be heard alongside those of the victims.

Reflections on Art Poem 2
I look,
    I see,
    I listen,
    and draw conclusions.

Reflections on Art 3
After I reach a conclusion
    I reopen the discussion.
    My mind cannot stay silent
    for fear of letting tyranny in.

Reflections on Art 5
I came I saw I felt
    I imagined and drew
    ink words that composed
    pictures in my mind
    with no precedent
    and no pretence.

Reflections on Art 7
On the road through life
    I cherish my childhood
    and then my youth
    to nourish the man
    as he grows through life
    filled with ideas
    and new imaginings
    facing the world's winds.

Reflections on Art 8
They run after art
    in the galleries
    for the galleries.
They are paid
    to look after
    our nation's collections.
    Do they use their power
    for art to flower
    or for themselves?
Artwork as pawns
    in a power play
    to manipulate, to blackmail.
And how long must I wait
    for these emperors
    to say hello?
What about Art?

ARCHITECTURE

To Be (an architect) Alive Today

Beyond the media-driven impression
    of happiness,
    the endless consumption and amassing
    of goods in the drawer,
    and where everything is measured by the
    growth of money,
    could enjoyment in everyday existence,
    in life, be valued more?
And how can we find these in the arts, rather
    than shops?
    If the intangibles of friendship, love and
    trust became the norm,
    how would we measure success through
    a new aesthetic
    of the unselfish when unselfishness rules
    after the reform?
Would we still have a need to celebrate the
    individual?
    Or is celebration and recognition
    essentially so human,
    distorted only by those who seek, not
    those who quietly accept.
    Is 'amuse ourselves to death' the only plan
    since time began?
The West reached a level of material well-
    being
    through its intense exploitation and
    control of earth's resource.
    But not content, man allowed unreason
    to wreak its wrath.
    Was this caused by unhappiness or a sign
    of nature's course?
Globalised competition to exploit what
    remains,
    has meant that we have all become the
    slaves of our technology,
    of the instruments that gave us such
    control,
    instead of becoming intelligent guardians
    of our ecology.

Technological innovation is not controlled
    even by the most advanced and
    sophisticated societies,
    whose legal and social structures are
    quite impotent
    in the face of global economic and
    political forces
These forces drive innovation, not the
    needs of man.
    Societies face their aged, brittle social
    institutions,
    designed for different times, and see
    them disappearing
    into an accelerating global vortex
    of executions.
Why, when we are older, do we see
    things more clearly?
    Is it that we begin to be alive
    in a different way?

    Eco_nomic man should seek
    to protect our biosphere
    with its beautiful cultures, not just seek
    so much fame and money.
Ironically, an economy based on
    competitive altruism,
    can give us and our planet growth
    and happiness in a new sense.
    It's good to be alive today, but
    as in all things,
    anticipatory planning will always
    be our best defence.

Management Madness

Client, Architect, Builder.
    It was a simple construct.
    My mind imagining, my hand drawing,
    engaging the client,
    then the maker, the builder.
Today, the management advice leviathan
    rides every sea of commerce and culture
    taking little or no responsibility
    from those
    who are supposed to carry responsibility,
    but who prefer the mirage of assurance,
    of reassurance, of independent project
    managers.

Thus, the advisor, the management
    consultants –
    our industry's own behemoth –
    burns the lands
    of creativity, makes weak the spirit
    of adventure,
    makes supine the client and impotent
    the architect.
If this is the process of refining wisdom
    that allows arrogance without knowledge
    or experience
    to suck our energy into a miasma
    of mediocrity
    we have only ourselves to blame.
Not screaming 'stop this absurdity,
    this draining of national resource,
    this irresponsibility, this mindless waste
    of money'.

Architecture

*"an infallible rule: a prince who is not himself wise
cannot be wisely advised...
good advice, wherever it comes from, depend
on the shrewdness of the prince
who seeks it, and not the shrewdness of the
prince on good advice".
(The Prince, Nicollo Machiavelli, 1513)*

Is the reason that management advisers have so
much influence with so little, that the
recipient doesn't know what is really
needed?

It's an end game.
   You can't see it until it's there.
   Only imagine.
And when it's there
   you can't do any more
   except watch people ignoring
   architecture – walking straight past,
   head down
   into the one beautiful piece of work
   that is unexpectedly positioned.

British Empire, British Mire

London was an outpost of the Roman Empire
    and we preserve this heritage below
    ground.
London was the centre of the British Empire
    and we're reminded everywhere above
    ground.
Many would like architects to design
    in a manner
    that is reminiscent of one or the other.

A Lost Past for a Future

We speculate on the past,
    upon knowledge lost.
    We recall how Brunelleschi
    went to Rome to learn and see
    the lost construction art.
The world of structures,
    a world full of ideas
    that shared its learning
    in the effort of building
    man's creativity and art.
Today, I look around and see
    architects so busy
    yet so lost in their self
    without a social belief
    and a shallow sense of art.

I see a new paradigm
> one that leans on time
> of past architecture
> that wanted to share
> its values – social art.

Do we have the desire
> to recapture higher
> values of a society,
> to be really free?
> Responsible art?

Architecture without values
> cannot reanimate the dead body.
> If we can clean the air,
> and stem the rising sea
> our architecture will mean
> we have once more an art.

Environment matters.
> But in a society in tatters
> what good is the pv cell
> when we are living in hell?
> The art of Living is the real art.

An architecture to make
> us smile, to laugh and
> to know the world is OK
> that people have shelter
> that we have learned to share.

OUR PLANET

I Long for the Ocean

I long for the ocean
    where the sea meets the land
    and my footsteps vanish,
    traceless in the sand.
I run into the foaming sea
    as it crashes and rushes to the dune
    during the night. It catches
    fractured moons, the moon.
Below the water undercurrents
    stir the colours of the sky,
    the depth of the ocean
    dark blue where I lie.
Blue is the colour chosen by
    many, the hue of our dreams
    the favourite of Miro and
    Klein's ultramarine.

The blue air of the horizon slips
    between air and water, both blue,
    dissolving Earth's gorgeous sky,
    with much beauty too.
The ocean flows all around us
    like the wind and the air
    for us to feel wrapped in love,
    carried in blueness, everywhere.

The Arctic

I saw and felt a country
    grand, yet people sad,
    standing on a slice of ice
    watching the throw of the dice
    that gave Inuits a bad
    turn.
Arctic tern
    sweeping over seeping ice
    organic flurries
    sighted beneath waves, the tern,
    journeys the earth to return
    disturbed, and that worries
    man.

Fall

I lie here in the stillness of the night,
    a shadow movement of the moonlight
    on the white plastered wall,
    and listening to a leaf fall.
I sense microbes moving upon my skin
    far exceeding the number of stars
    within a galaxy
    and the neurons I can't see.
And nature's marvellous diversity
    takes us forward, informs our artistry
    to help create our dreams,
    and our nightmares too, it seems.

*a poem of time *

The sunlight moves, fast.
    We think the sun's still,
    and that we are being cast
    around it.
But we think, slowly,
    of time's past as if
    it were linear only,
    future-past.
As we think, we know.
    But then realise
    that we do not know time, no,
    nothing's firm.

Everything is timed.
    But time is nothing,
    a misplaced idea, a chimed
    enclosure.
Prisoners of tic-toc, of the sunrise, sunset
    too, of a strange photonic
    energy.
Life has its season.
    Not time going forward
    or backward, nor a reason,
    a cycle.

Non-Linearity

There is something remarkable
    about non-linearity.
Not only is it beautiful
    and presents nature's beauty to us,
    the scintillating light dancing upon waves
    of water flowing with the pull of the
    moon,
    the veined lime white, green, yellow, purple
    and red of leaves preparing to fall,
    but it is also part of the autumn of life
    when things don't flow sequentially
    anymore,
    but go up and down, unpredictably,
    and without any temporal constancy.
Is this how we age?
    Birthdays don't follow one another
    because they don't matter anymore.

Landscape

The calyx is made up of sepals.
The corolla is made up of petals.
The androecium is made up of stamens.
The gynoecium is made up of carpels.
The landscape became sere and yellow
    dried and withered
        desert future below the sierra.

Chemical Engineering 2
(a scribble about the way we are)

Nature developed from a firmament,
    from a cocktail of chemicals, that
    eventually processed themselves through
    amino acids
    and a multitude of molecules
    into a vast array of vegetable, mineral
    and animal wonders
    that became our Earth, our house,
    our home.
At some point in nature's processing,
    memory occurred.
    A protein that replicated – a form
    of memory,
    a chemical memory that eventually
    began investigating
    its world and itself.

The memory developed imagination
    and reason,
    and a logic that produced a revolution
    that became a manipulation of nature
    by one of its own,
    man, solely for man, who metamorphosed
    into unreason,
    consumption for consumption.
One day he woke up, slowly, to find that
    his house was his home, and it was the
    only one available.
    And that too many people were living in it
    without a common creed or ethos.
    The vast majority were oblivious
    to the rotting stinking home it was turning
    into.

Was there a flood once, or is there one
    coming?
    Will it put out the fires, will it clean
    the mess.
    Until we are in front of the catastrophe
    we appear capable only of arguing, stealing
    from each other,
    competing for greed and fighting.
    Are we able to slow down for a while
    and to reconsider what we are doing?
Everything is connected.
    Our domestic economy is the wrong one.
    It needs to be created around a competitive
    altruism,
    that will hurt nothing but begin mending
    our home.

An economy built upon the new chemical
    engineering
    learnt from nature and applied to benefit
    our well-being,
    rather than our being, our self-interest.
We have a choice to share values
    or value shares.
    At the moment the world still
    values shares,
    while I value the world.

Patterns 2, Part 1
(extreme scales of seeing extract)

The way we see reveals the world,
    the way we make art feels the world,
    and the way we think peels the world.
Now man has extended eyes,
    the world produces even greater surprise
    unfurled through the next Nobel Prize.
James Webb macroscope out there
    and photon microscope in here
    and these new eyes give hope so clear.

Patterns 2, Part 2
(at the large scale – extract)

We inhabit a planet that orbits
    a modest size star that sits
    in an anonymous blackish sea
    of a modest size galaxy.
    Just one of a thousand billion
    galaxies from blue to vermillion
    in this beautiful universe.
This James Webb is a time machine,
    the latest 'look-back' that can glean
    time before time before time
    into deep space and the sublime,
    when expanded cooling gas gave rise
    to galaxies, stars, planets, and skies,
    for our eyes and minds to create
    modest projects deemed so great.

Patterns 2, Part 3
(at the small scale – extract)

Similarly, at the microscopic scale,
    we can detect a spectacular trail
    of energy flows and a pattern
    here and there, miniature rings of Saturn.
And at the sub-atomic level, chaotic
    and unnatural implants in our neurotic
    homes etched with products we do not need,
    nor desire, if we had much less greed.
Understanding the world, making sense
    in a cosmos so miniscule, and so dense,
    does require patterns and geometries
    to provide us with a handle upon the seas
    of movement that make life so vital.
I sense science has no truck with ornament,
    using patterns to better describe
    the natural world and the human tribe.

Man rearranges some bones or stones,
    produces helical graphite, crashes electrons
    in a particle accelerator, throws paint
    at a wall,
    or writes an article – he shows that
    he's in thrall.
To open a stone, microscopically, is to reveal
    its atomic
    and molecular pattern; so the stone
    is nature's trick,
    to be caressed to allow the wave
    of memories
    to surface upon the visible stony mess
    as stories.

Silence once again

I have watched
    but never heard
    spider threading,
    spider weaving.
I have watched
    but never heard
    butterflying
    flapping, kissing.

Raining 2012

A wet bank holiday
    watching the rain fall,
    the birds getting wet,
    and flowers hanging their heads
    under dripping branches.
A long weekend raining
    tears – all now history
    as the water runs away.
My heart was heavy too
    for the soul journeys
    you have travelled
    these last few days.
We can be permitted
    a moments melancholy
    from time to time
    as we hear the Earth cry.

Remembering the Skelligs

Floating past Little Skellig
    guano stained sandstone shelves
    screaming with gannets
    challenging themselves.
The blizzard sight of folded
    white wings, golden crown
    swashing into the sea
    eyes sharp bearing down.
Embarking at Skellig Michael
    the bigger of the twins
    climbed to the beehives
    past a thousand puffins.
Painted grey scaled gannet isle
    and magic puffin rock
    where their tasty young
    attract the gannet flock.

Amazing forms, beautiful stones
    resistant to weather
    from the Atlantic
    harbours for the feather.
We cannot change the shape of
    the blue ocean or sky,
    just wonder, wander
    indulging the mind's eye.

COVID

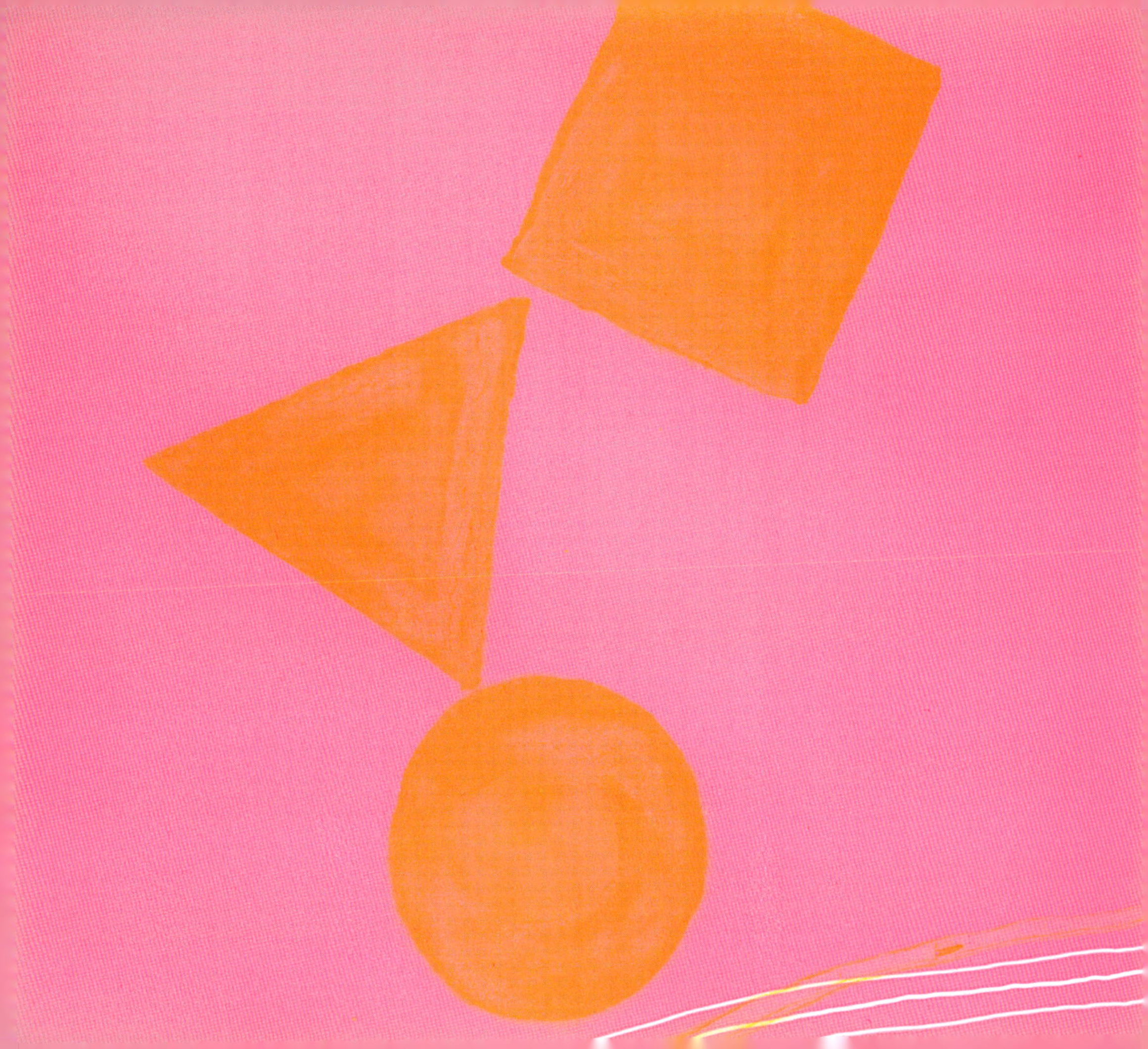

Elysium

From Elysium to Delirium …
    a time of reflection,
    solitude and isolation.
When nature reasserts itself
    upon our imagination.
Now is different from then,
    and then again, the same.

Heartsearing

That was heartsearing – …
    pricked eyes and gulps of air;
    and so chilling to see
    all those empty streets
    in all the major capitals.
    It felt like a requiem
    for the souls of the living.

Come isolate with me.

Can anyone understand
    how beautiful it is to be alone
    and to listen to nature's voice
    where every sound is heard
    as when a leaf or snowflake falls
    upon the Earth, and is heard
    vibrating through the magma
    to be sensed on the other side?
That wavelength of sound,
    spherical twin of light beam
    each sending their word
    of love to the world,
    and to the cosmos
    in which we spin and fly,
    in the web of the universe's
    majestic timeless explosion.

In this world and the next,
    recognising how beautiful
    isolation can be when we
    cannot be alone, when
    the waves of sound and light
    are forever chattering
    if only we will listen,
    and hear their wisdom.
There is a child
    in everyone,
    throughout life,
    enduring and aching
    when love is denied,
    a mother or father absent,
    forever crying
    into the emotionless dirt.

Christmas 2020

A Christmas without you,
    and it's the first in fifty years.
    Christmas is for the child in us,
    the laughter and the tears.
Thinking of you alone
    in a room full of flashing lights
    and those electronic signals
    pulsing through your strange nights.
As your bloodied, bruised mind
    begins to heal, synapses form
    anew recovering functions
    lost during that brainstorm.
Christmas is with you and
    the excited child beneath the tree,
    and you talking and playing,
    being here and carefree.

Limboland

Love seems inexhaustible as if there are no
 boundaries between us as singular beings,
 and where art is the expression
 of loneliness, love is the opposite.
Looking for words to describe this limboland
 …
 floating on a stormy sea as one wave rises
 with hope, only to fold over
 and to avoid being beneath its power,
 surfacing to breathe
 as it pulses relentlessly with the cosmos.

Like my creative world,
 the singular art and the plural architecture,
 the one and the collective;
 the scientific logic and the emotional
 expression,
 on the crest of a wave, surfing
 without falling,
 finding equilibrium at the edge of now.

WAR & PEACE

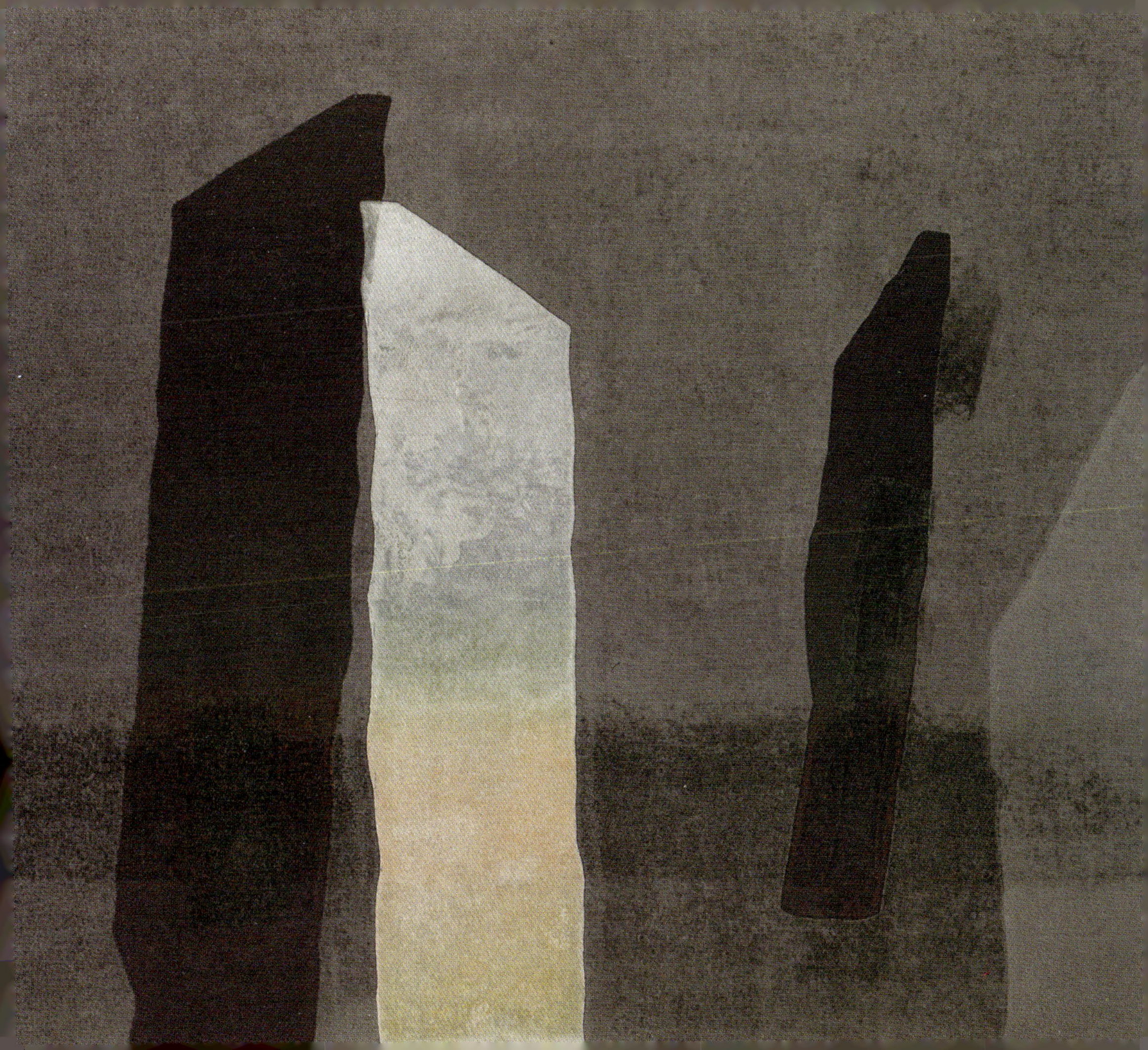

No War

No.
    No more,
    no more war,
    and
    let our hearts
    accept
    war
    is dead.

Fardels of War

Time
    to dump
    the fardels
    of myths
    of battles and heroes.
They are but
    collections of violence,
    'tis time to grow up.
There are others
    of love
    and peace.

Give me a Spade

Give me a spade
    and I'll dig deeper
    for love than anyone.
Show me your face,
    and I will tender
    a kiss 'til the dawn sun.

Nature's Confetti

How strange it is that winter
    humans are adding layers of fur
    while I enjoy rich nature's confetti
    on this beautiful clear morning
    watching trees and plants shedding
    their garments to meet winter naked.
They will sleep as we stay awake,
    hibernating white winter's break
    and give heat to keep us warm.
    While shaking their rainbow leaves
    I sense the cold wind increasing,
    hurling white clouds across the sky.

Skin

You spoke of skin,
    of darker skin,
    maybe of lighter skin.
    But I am blind
    and cannot see your skin.

Summer 2012

Welcome sun and rain
    to lawn and glade.
    We brought our fork, our
    trowel and spade.
Now we smile as buds open,
    and vegetables soften,
    and fruits ripen
    in our secret garden.
We build the walls
    to enclose this paradise
    and insert a door
    to be entered twice?

LOST FRIENDS

Andreas in Berlin

Spalling graffitied concrete wall
    whose rusting bars bent
    and twisted and which secretly
    pulled at aching hearts torn apart.
This red blood rusty opaque screen
    turned into cold stainless steel sheet
    that divides and protects nothing,
    obscures and hides our stupidity,
    and in the night's cloudy blanket
    two candles flicker in the distance and
    melt the dark emptiness into silence,
    this silence into thoughts
    that will keep memories precious
    within the beautiful walled garden of our
    minds.

And let our heart sigh
    as we try to sleep
    wrapped in disbelief
    and images of a love
    a voice, a smile, a laugh,
    the shape of a lip, a kiss
    a caress, the outline of a finger,
    the texture of a hand, and
    thoughts that never end as
    we prepare to fold and pack so gently
    those waves of energy that will forever
    sparkle as a message from the stars
    against the black ink of time.

Dead Ground

The horizon, dark, dead ground,
    sea of dead grass
    before a dawn-lit tilted arc,
    roots of nature and men all around.
Is this my bed, dark, dead ground?
    Mud of white mass,
    bodies gone, unlit night, sky-lark
    chirps, a warbling, timing silent sound.
A distant bridge, gone dead ground,
    gone the marsh gas
    fresh air, I hear a dog bark,
    sound of living souls.
I am homebound.

Alec

(on the death of dear Alec Finn, Galway, Ireland
– for his wife Leonie)

A beautiful life,
    Strong man, bird of prey,
    a sunrise, quiet green bay
    of nature, deep love.
Such colourful autumns
    of music and flames,
    a gorgeous sunset claims
    the castle's window.
A star burns and yet
    the pitch-dark night comes
    as cold emptiness drums
    our sad hearts tonight,
    and tomorrow night.
Loneliness holds the soul
    aching in the black hole
    left by his going.
Where? Crossing the bay,
    arcing through the sky?
Somewhere, you, bird, fly high
    Sharp eye, twinkling again.

Night Sky,
To John Hoyland. Mysteries catalogue, 2011

I waited for the cosmic wind
    to touch my face,
    when it did, I looked again
    into a different place.
The starry sky is fleeing now
    to stage a dance
    in deep blue, beyond the Plough
    another chance to glance.
John imagined the waves of time
    as blue swept spaces
    that curve deep into the mind
    to race to other places.
I dived to join the dancing light
    to hold one white
    star of fiery ice real tight.
    Ah, Vincent, coloured night
of crescent moon, clouds roll,
    from star to star,
    an unlit, dark cypress hole
    stretches space. Au revoir.

Nanni's Funeral

Heaven's blue sky
    managed to shed a few angels' tears
    that stripped the warmth
    off yesterday's sun.
A simple day
    charged with bells of memory.
    we sang, prayed and
    walked the final path
    to throw roses and petals
    into the void.
This day in Picardy was special
    and important, for it was here,
    her and him set me sailing
    the seas of design,
    clients who trusted me,
    Bohem-Ian, without question.
A rare gift to anyone.
    I took it, smiled and delivered.
    The rest became my life
    away from death's day today.

Dear Hinnerk

To Hinnerk Wehberg, Landscape Architect, Hamburg

May the geometry of snowflakes
    grow like leaves in your bank balance,
    and the softness of unfrozen water
    irrigate the deep deserted channels
    of your mind to bring forth ideas
    that you never knew you had.

Oh Europe

After the wake,
    the all-consuming sadness
    envelops as a cold mist
    as we say farewell to a beautiful idea –
    of common bonds and friendship
    across the water that connects us all,
    but also divides through minds that cannot see,
    of consonance between peoples and nations,
    of a determination to deliver peace forever
    to a continent blooded by endless wars.
It is such a brilliant idea but was not
    of Britain's making.
    It happened in spite of us
    and I fear that the English spite and
    its misplaced pride will ultimately weaken us,
    and Europe.

Dark Blanket for Mick Moon

Our imagined hands rested on a shared surface
    of laughter, conversation, good food and
    deep red wine,
    and when your hand lay on Mick's
    shoulder
    brought back his smiling face.
The strange but common grey-blue sky
    rests above you, and for all your friends,
    now, like a dark blanket in the snow
    you can but question why.
But we who feel love and loss
    throughout our days must tender
    our care for every moment of life,
    as those parting clouds cross.

On Nature's Dying

A fading flower is no reason to mourn,
    nor dying autumn leaves, –
    for nature has no melancholy
    in time passing, or in gravity.

Published in 2024
by Unicorn
an imprint of
Unicorn Publishing Group
Charleston Studio
Meadow Business Centre
Lewes BN8 5RW
www.unicornpublishing.org

Text and Images
© Ian Ritchie

ritchie studio

All rights reserved.
No part of the contents of this book may be reproduced, stored in or introduced into a retrieval system, or transmitted, in any form or by any means (electronic, mechanical, photocopying, recording or otherwise), without the prior written permission of the copyright holder and the above publisher of this book.

Every effort has been made to trace copyright holders and to obtain their permission for the use of copyrighted material. The publisher apologises for any errors or omissions and would be grateful to be notified of any corrections that should be incorporated in future reprints or editions of this book.

ISBN 978-1-916846-43-2
10 9 8 7 6 5 4 3 2 1 0

Designed and typeset in Monotype Centaur by corvo-uk.com
Printed in Riga by Finetone Ltd

IMAGES

Front cover:	*Arctic Warming 3*
Front endpaper:	*Arctic Warming 4*
Back endpaper:	*Arctic Warming 1*
Youth:	*Study in Curved Light 2*
Love:	*Fish and the Moon 3*
Art:	*Study in Light 2*
Architecture:	*Study in Light 3*
Our Planet:	*Stenness Stones 15*
Covid:	*Disequilibrium*
War & Peace:	*Stenness Stones 12*
Lost Friends:	*Arctic Imagined 4*